Sketches of Southern life

Frances E. Watkins Harper

Originally Published by
Ferguson Bros. & Co., Printers
1891

Contents

AUNT CHLOE.	1
The Deliverance.	3
Aunt Chloe's Politics.	7
Learning to Read.	9
Church Building.	11
The Reunion.	13
"I THIRST."	15
First Voice.	15
Second Voice.	15
THE DYING QUEEN.	17
THE JEWISH GRANDFATHER'S STORY.	19
SHALMANEZER, *PRINCE OF COSMAN*.	23
OUT IN THE COLD.	31
SAVE THE BOYS.	33
NOTHING AND SOMETHING.	35
WANDERER'S RETURN.	37
"FISHERS OF MEN."	39
SIGNING THE PLEDGE.	41

AUNT CHLOE.

I remember, well remember, That dark and dreadful day, When they whispered to me, "Chloe, Your children's sold away!"

It seemed as if a bullet Had shot me through and through, And I felt as if my heart-strings Was breaking right in two.

And I says to cousin Milly, "There must be some mistake; Where's Mistus?" "In the great house crying—" Crying like her heart would break.

"And the lawyer's there with Mistus; Says he's come to 'ministrate, 'Cause when master died he just left Heap of debt on the estate.

"And I thought 'twould do you good To bid your boys good-bye—" To kiss them both and shake their hands, And have a hearty cry.

"Oh! Chloe, I knows how you feel, 'Cause I'se been through it all; I thought my poor old heart would break, When master sold my Saul."

Just then I heard the footsteps Of my children at the door, And I rose right up to meet them, But I fell upon the floor.

And I heard poor Jakey saying, "Oh, mammy, don't you cry!" And I felt my children kiss me And bid me, both, good-bye.

Then I had a mighty sorrow, Though I nursed it all alone; But I wasted to a shadow, And turned to skin and bone.

But one day dear Uncle Jacob (In heaven he's now a saint) Said, "Your poor heart is in the fire, But child you must not faint."

Then I said to Uncle Jacob, If I was good like you, When the heavy trouble dashed me I'd know just what to do.

Then he said to me, "Poor Chloe, The way is open wide:" And he told me of the Saviour, And the fountain in His side.

Then he said "Just take your burden To the blessed Master's feet; I takes all my troubles, Chloe, Right unto the mercy-seat."

His words waked up my courage, And I began to pray, And I felt my heavy burden Rolling like a stone away.

And a something seemed to tell me, You will see your boys again—" And that hope was like a poultice Spread upon a dreadful pain.

And it often seemed to whisper, Chloe, trust and never fear; You'll get justice in the kingdom, If you do not get it here.

The Deliverance.

Master only left old Mistus One bright and handsome boy; But she fairly doted on him, He was her pride and joy.

We all liked Mister Thomas, He was so kind at heart; And when the young folks got in scrapes, He always took their part.

He kept right on that very way Till he got big and tall, And old Mistus used to chide him, And say he'd spile us all.

But somehow the farm did prosper When he took things in hand; And though all the servants liked him, He made them understand.

One evening Mister Thomas said, "Just bring my easy shoes: I am going to sit by mother, And read her up the news."

Soon I heard him tell old Mistus "We're bound to have a fight; But we'll whip the Yankees, mother, We'll whip them sure as night!"

Then I saw old Mistus tremble; She gasped and held her breath; And she looked on Mister Thomas With a face as pale as death.

"They are firing on Fort Sumpter; Oh! I wish that I was there!" Why, dear mother! what's the matter? You're the picture of despair."

"I was thinking, dearest Thomas, 'Twould break my very heart If a fierce and dreadful battle Should tear our lives apart."

"None but cowards, dearest mother, Would skulk unto the rear, When the tyrant's hand is shaking, All the heart is holding dear."

I felt sorry for old Mistus; She got too full to speak; But I saw the great big tear-drops A running down her cheek.

Mister Thomas too was troubled With choosing on that night, Betwixt staying with his mother And joining in the fight.

Soon down into the village came A call for volunteers; Mistus gave up Mister Thomas, With many sighs and tears.

His uniform was real handsome; He looked so brave and strong; But somehow I couldn't help thinking His fighting must be wrong.

Though the house was very lonesome, I thought 'twould all come right, For I felt somehow or other We was mixed up in that fight.

And I said to Uncle Jacob, "Now old Mistus feels the sting, For this parting with your children Is a mighty dreadful thing."

"Never mind," said Uncle Jacob, "Just wait and watch and pray, For I feel right sure and certain, Slavery's bound to pass away;

"Because I asked the Spirit, If God is good and just, How it happened that the masters Did grind us to the dust.

"And something reasoned right inside, Such should not always be; And you could not beat it out my head, The Spirit spoke to me."

And his dear old eyes would brighten, And his lips put on a smile, Saying, "Pick up faith and courage, And just wait a little while."

Mistus prayed up in the parlor, That the Secesh all might win; We were praying in the cabins, Wanting freedom to begin.

Mister Thomas wrote to Mistus, Telling 'bout the Bull's Run fight, That his troops had whipped the Yankees And put them all to flight.

Mistus' eyes did fairly glisten; She laughed and praised the South, But I thought some day she'd laugh On tother side her mouth.

I used to watch old Mistus' face, And when it looked quite long I would say to Cousin Milly, The battle's going wrong;

Not for us, but for the Rebels," My heart 'would fairly skip, When Uncle Jacob used to say, "The North is bound to whip."

And let the fight go as it would—" Let North or South prevail—" He always kept his courage up, And never let it fail.

And he often used to tell us, "Children, don't forget to pray; For the darkest time of morning Is just 'fore the break of day."

Well, one morning bright and early We heard the fife and drum, And the booming of the cannon—" The Yankee troops had come.

When the word ran through the village, The colored folks are free—" In the kitchens and the cabins We held a jubilee.

When they told us Mister Lincoln Said that slavery was dead, We just poured our prayers and blessings Upon his precious head.

We just laughed, and danced, and shouted, And prayed, and sang, and cried, And we thought dear Uncle Jacob Would fairly crack his side.

But when old Mistus heard it, She groaned and hardly spoke; When she had to lose her servants, Her heart was almost broke.

'Twas a sight to see our people Going out, the troops to meet, Almost dancing to the music, And marching down the street.

After years of pain and parting, Our chains was broke in two, And we was so mighty happy, We didn't know what to do.

But we soon got used to freedom, Though the way at first was rough; But we weathered through the tempest, For slavery made us tough.

But we had one awful sorrow, It almost turned my head, When a mean and wicked cretur Shot Mister Lincoln dead.

'Twas a dreadful solemn morning, I just staggered on my feet; And the women they were crying And screaming in the street.

But if many prayers and blessings Could bear him to the throne, I should think when Mister Lincoln died, That heaven just got its own.

Then we had another President,—" What do you call his name? Well, if the colored folks forget him They wouldn't be much to blame.

We thought he'd be the Moses Of all the colored race; But when the Rebels pressed us hard He never showed his face.

But something must have happened him, Right curi's I'll be bound, 'Cause I heard 'em talking 'bout a circle That he was swinging round.

But everything will pass away—" He went like time and tide—" And when the next election came They let poor Andy slide.

But now we have a President, And if I was a man I'd vote for him for breaking up The wicked Ku-Klux Klan.

And if any man should ask me If I would sell my vote, I'd tell him I was not the one To change and turn my coat;

If freedom seem'd a little rough I'd weather through the gale; And as to buying up my vote, I hadn't it for sale.

I do not think I'd ever be As slack as Jonas Handy; Because I heard he sold his vote For just three sticks of candy.

But when John Thomas Reeder brought His wife some flour and meat, And told her he had sold his vote For something good to eat.

You ought to seen Aunt Kitty raise, And heard her blaze away; She gave the meat and flour a toss, And said they should not stay.

And I should think he felt quite cheap For voting the wrong side; And when Aunt Kitty scolded him, He just stood up and cried.

But the worst fooled man I ever saw, Was when poor David Rand Sold out for flour and sugar; The sugar was mixed with sand.

I'll tell you how the thing got out; His wife had company, And she thought the sand was sugar, And served it up for tea.

When David sipped and sipped the tea, Somehow it didn't taste right; I guess when he found he was sipping sand, He was mad enough to fight.

The sugar looked so nice and white—" It was spread some inches deep—" But underneath was a lot of sand; Such sugar is mighty cheap.

You'd laughed to seen Lucinda Grange Upon her husband's track; When he sold his vote for rations She made him take 'em back.

Day after day did Milly Green Just follow after Joe, And told him if he voted wrong To take his rags and go.

I think that Curnel Johnson said His side had won the day, Had not we women radicals Just got right in the way.

And yet I would not have you think That all our men are shabby; But 'tis said in every flock of sheep There will be one that's scabby.

I've heard, before election came They tried to buy John Slade; But he gave them all to understand That he wasn't in that trade.

And we've got lots of other men Who rally round the cause, And go for holding up the hands That gave us equal laws.

Who know their freedom cost too much Of blood and pain and treasure, For them to fool away their votes For profit or for pleasure.

Aunt Chloe's Politics.

Of course, I don't know very much About these politics, But I think that some who run 'em, Do mighty ugly tricks.

I've seen 'em honey-fugle round, And talk so awful sweet, That you'd think them full of kindness, As an egg is full of meat.

Now I don't believe in looking Honest people in the face, And saying when you're doing wrong, That "I haven't sold my race."

When we want to school our children, If the money isn't there, Whether black or white have took it, The loss we all must share.

And this buying up each other Is something worse than mean, Though I thinks a heap of voting, I go for voting clean.

Learning to Read.

Very soon the Yankee teachers Came down and set up school; But, oh! how the Rebs did hate it,—" It was agin' their rule.

Our masters always tried to hide Book learning from our eyes; Knowledge didn't agree with slavery—" 'Twould make us all too wise.

But some of us would try to steal A little from the book, And put the words together, And learn by hook or crook.

I remember Uncle Caldwell, Who took pot-liquor fat And greased the pages of his book, And hid it in his hat.

And had his master ever seen The leaves upon his head, He'd have thought them greasy papers, But nothing to be read.

And there was Mr. Turner's Ben, Who heard the children spell, And picked the words right up by heart, And learned to read 'em well.

Well, the Northern folks kept sending The Yankee teachers down; And they stood right up and helped us, Though Rebs did sneer and frown.

And, I longed to read my Bible, For precious words it said; But when I begun to learn it, Folks just shook their heads,

And said there is no use trying, Oh! Chloe, you're too late; But as I was rising sixty, I had no time to wait.

So I got a pair of glasses, And straight to work I went, And never stopped till I could read The hymns and Testament.

Then I got a little cabin A place to call my own—" And I felt as independent As the queen upon her throne.

Church Building.

Uncle Jacob often told us, Since freedom blessed our race We ought all to come together And build a meeting place.

So we pinched, and scraped, and spared, A little here and there: Though our wages was but scanty, The church did get a share.

And, when the house was finished, Uncle Jacob came to pray; He was looking mighty feeble, And his head was awful gray.

But his voice rang like a trumpet; His eyes looked bright and young; And it seemed a mighty power Was resting on his tongue.

And he gave us all his blessing— 'Twas parting words he said, For soon we got the message The dear old man was dead.

But I believe he's in the kingdom, For when we shook his hand He said, "Children, you must meet me Right in the promised land;

"For when I'm done a moiling And toiling here below, Through the gate into the city Straightway I hope to go."

The Reunion.

Well, one morning real early I was going down the street, And I heard a stranger asking For Missis Chloe Fleet.

There was a something in his voice That made me feel quite shaky, And when I looked right in his face, Who should it be but Jakey!

I grasped him tight, and took him home—" What gladness filled my cup! And I laughed, and just rolled over, And laughed, and just give up.

"Where have you been? O Jakey, dear! Why didn't you come before? Oh! when you children went away My heart was awful sore."

"Why, mammy, I've been on your hunt Since ever I've been free, And I have heard from brother Ben," "He's down in Tennessee.

"He wrote me that he had a wife." "And children?" "Yes, he's three." "You married, too?" "Oh no, indeed, I thought I'd first get free."

"Then, Jakey, you will stay with me, And comfort my poor heart; Old Mistus got no power now To tear us both apart.

"I'm richer now than Mistus, Because I have got my son; And Mister Thomas he is dead, And she's got nary one.

"You must write to brother Benny That he must come this fall, And we'll make the cabin bigger, And that will hold us all.

"Tell him I want to see 'em all Before my life do cease: And then, like good old Simeon, I hope to die in peace."

"I THIRST."

First Voice.

I thirst, but earth cannot allay The fever coursing through my veins, The healing stream is far away— It flows through Salem's lovely plains.

The murmurs of its crystal flow Break ever o'er this world of strife; My heart is weary, let me go, To bathe it in the stream of life;

For many worn and weary hearts Have bathed in this pure healing stream, And felt their griefs and cares depart, E'en like some sad forgotten dream.

Second Voice.

"The Word is nigh thee, even in thy heart."

Say not, within thy weary heart, Who shall ascend above, To bring unto thy fever'd lips The fount of joy and love.

Nor do thou seek to vainly delve Where death's pale angels tread, To hear the murmur of its flow Around the silent dead.

Within, in thee is one living fount, Fed from the springs above; There quench thy thirst till thou shalt bathe In God's own sea of love.

THE DYING QUEEN.

"I would meet death awake."

The strength that bore her on for years Was ebbing fast away, And o'er the pale and life-worn face, Death's solemn shadows lay.

With tender love and gentle care, Friends gathered round her bed, And for her sake each footfall hushed The echoes of its tread.

They knew the restlessness of death Through every nerve did creep, And carefully they tried to lull The dying Queen to sleep.

In vain she felt Death's icy hand Her failing heart-strings shake; And, rousing up, she firmly said, "I'd meet my God awake."

Awake, I've met the battle's shock, And born the cares of state; Nor shall I take your lethean cup, And slumber at death's gate.

Did I not watch with eyes alert, The path where foes did tend; And shall I veil my eyes with sleep, To meet my God and friend?

Nay, rather from my weary lids, This heavy slumber shake, That I may pass the mystic vale, And meet my God awake.

THE JEWISH GRANDFATHER'S STORY.

Come, gather around me, children, And a story I will tell. How we built the beautiful temple— The temple we love so well.

I must date my story backward To a distant age and land, When God did break our fathers' chains By his mighty outstretched hand

Our fathers were strangers and captives, Where the ancient Nile doth flow; Smitten by cruel taskmasters, And burdened by toil and woe.

As a shepherd, to pastures green Doth lead with care his sheep, So God divided the great Red Sea, And led them through the deep.

You've seen me plant a tender vine, And guard it with patient care, Till its roots struck in the mellow earth, And it drank the light and air.

So God did plant our chosen race, As a vine in this fair land; And we grew and spread a fruitful tree, The planting of his right hand.

The time would fail strove I to tell, All the story of our race— Of our grand old leader, Moses, And Joshua in his place,

Of all our rulers and judges, From Joshua unto Saul, Over whose doomed and guilty head Fell ruin and death's dark pall.

Of valiant Jephthah, whose brave heart With sudden grief did bow, When his daughter came with dance and song Unconscious of his vow.

Of Gideon, lifting up his voice To him who rules the sky, And wringing out his well drenched fleece, When all around was dry.

How Deborah, 'neath her spreading palms, A judge in Israel rose, And wrested victory from the hands Of Jacob's heathen foes.

Of Samuel, an upright judge. The last who ruled our tribes, Whose noble life and cleanly hands, Were pure and free from bribes.

Of David, with his checkered life Our tuneful minstrel king, Who breathed in sadness and delight, The psalms we love to sing.

Of Solomon, whose wandering heart, From Jacob's God did stray, And cast the richest gifts of life, In pleasure's cup away.

How aged men advised his son, But found him weak and vain, Until the kingdom from his hands Was rudely rent in twain.

Oh! sin and strife are fearful things, They widen as they go, And leave behind them shades of death, And open gates of woe.

A trail of guilt, a gloomy line, Ran through our nation's life, And wicked kings provoked our God, And sin and woe were rife.

At length, there came a day of doom— A day of grief and dread; When judgment like a fearful storm Swept o'er our country's head.

And we were captives many years, Where Babel's stream doth flow; With harps unstrung, on willows hung, We wept in silent woe.

We could not sing the old, sweet songs, Our captors asked to hear; Our hearts were full, how could we sing The songs to us so dear?

As one who dreams a mournful dream, Which fades, as wanes the night, So God did change our gloomy lot From darkness into light.

Belshazzar in his regal halls, A sumptuous feast did hold; He praised his gods and drank his wine From sacred cups of gold.

When dance and song and revelry Had filled with mirth each hall, Belshazzar raised his eyes and saw A writing on the wall.

He saw, and horror blanched his cheek, His lips were white with fear; To read the words he quickly called For wise men, far and near.

But baffled seers, with anxious doubt Stood silent in the room, When Daniel came, a captive youth, And read the words of doom.

That night, within his regal hall, Belshazzar lifeless lay; The Persians grasped his fallen crown, And with the Mede held sway.

Darius came, and Daniel rose A man of high renown; But wicked courtiers schemed and planned To drag the prophet down.

They came as men who wished to place Great honors on their king— With flattering lips and oily words, Desired a certain thing.

They knew that Daniel, day by day Towards Salem turned his face, And asked the king to sign a law His hands might not erase.

That till one moon had waned away, No cherished wish or thing Should any ask of men or Gods, Unless it were the king.

But Daniel, full of holy trust, His windows opened wide, Regardless of the king's command, Unto his God he cried.

They brought him forth that he might be The hungry lion's meat, Awe struck, the lions turned away And crouched anear his feet.

The God he served was strong to save His servant in the den; The fate devised for Daniel's life O'er took those scheming men.

And Cyrus came, a gracious king, And gave the blest command, That we, the scattered Jews, should build Anew our fallen land.

The men who hated Juda's weal Were filled with bitter rage, And 'gainst the progress of our work Did evil men engage.

Sanballat tried to hinder us, And Gashmu uttered lies, But like a thing of joy and light, We saw our temple rise.

THE JEWISH GRANDFATHER'S STORY.

And from the tower of Hananeel Unto the corner gate, We built the wall and did restore The places desolate.

Some mocked us as we labored on And scoffingly did say, "If but a fox climb on the wall, Their work will give away."

But Nehemiah wrought in hope, Though heathen foes did frown "My work is great," he firmly said, "And I cannot come down."

And when Shemai counselled him The temple door to close, To hide, lest he should fall a prey Unto his cruel foes.

Strong in his faith, he answered, "No, He would oppose the tide, Should such as he from danger flee, And in the temple hide?"

We wrought in earnest faith and hope Until we built the wall, And then, unto a joyful feast Did priest and people call.

We came to dedicate the wall With sacrifice and joy— A happy throng, from aged sire Unto the fair-haired boy.

Our lips so used to mournful songs, Did joyous laughter fill, And strong men wept with sacred joy To stand on Zion's hill.

Mid scoffing foes and evil men, We built our city blest, And 'neath our sheltering vines and palms To-day in peace we rest.

SHALMANEZER, *PRINCE OF COSMAN.*

BY MRS. FRANCES E. W. HARPER.

Shalmanezer, Prince of Cosman, stood on the threshold of manly life, having just received a rich inheritance which had been left him by his father.

He was a magnificent-looking creature—the very incarnation of manly strength and beauty. The splendid poise of his limbs, the vigor and litheness of his motions, the glorious light that flashed from his splendid dark eyes, the bright joyous smiles that occasionally wreathed his fresh young lips, and the finely-erect carriage of his head, were enough to impress the beholder with the thought, "Here is an athlete armed for a glorious strife!"

While Shalmanezer was thinking upon his rich inheritance and how he should use it, he suddenly lifted his eyes and saw two strange-looking personages standing near him. They both advanced towards Shalmanezer when they saw their presence had attracted his attention.

The first one that approached the young man and addressed him, was named Desire. He was a pleasant-looking youth, with a flushed face, and eager, restless eyes. He looked as if he had been pursuing a journey, or had been grasping at an object he had failed to obtain. There was something in his manner that betrayed a want of rest—a look in his eyes which seemed to say, "I am not satisfied." But when he approached, he smiled in the most seductive manner, and, reaching out his hand to Shalmanezer said:

"I have come to welcome thee to man's estate, and for thy enjoyment, I have brought thee three friends who will lead thee into the brightest paths, and press to thy lips the sweetest elixirs."

Gladly the young man received the greeting of Desire, who immediately introduced his three companions, whose names were, Pleasure, Wealth, and Fame.—Pleasure was a most beautiful creature. Her lovely dark eyes flashed out a laughing light; upon her finely-carved lips hovered the brightest and sweetest smiles, which seemed ever ready to break into merry ripples of laughter; her robe was magnificently beautiful, as if it had imprisoned in its warp and woof the beauty of the rainbow and the glory of the setting sun;

in her hand she held a richly wrought chalice in which sparkled and effervesced a ruby-colored liquid which was as beautiful to the eye as it was pleasant to the taste. When Pleasure was presented to Shalmanezer, she held out to him her cup and said in the sweetest tones:

"Come, drink of my cup, it is sparkling and bright As rubies distilled in the morning light; A truce to sorrow and adieu to pain—" Here's the cup to strengthen, soothe and sustain."

Just as Shalmanezer was about to grasp the cup, the other personage approached him. Her name was Peace, and she was attended by a mild, earnest-looking young man called Self-Denial. In the calm depths of her dark-blue eyes was a tender, loving light, and on her brow a majestic serenity which seemed to say, "The cares of earth are at my feet; in vain its tempests sweep around my path." There was also a look of calm, grand patience on the brow of her attendant, which gave him the aspect of one who had passed through suffering unto Peace. Shalmanezer was gazing eagerly on the fair young face of Pleasure, and about to quaff the sparkling nectar, when Peace suddenly arrested his hand and exclaimed:

"Beware of this cup! 'Neath its ruddy glow, Is an undercurrent of shame and woe; 'Neath its sparkling sheen so fair and bright, Are serpents that hiss, and adders that bite."

The young man paused a moment, looked on the plain garb of Peace and then on the enchanting loveliness of Pleasure, and, pushing aside the hand of Peace with a scornful gesture, he said proudly and defiantly:

"I will follow Pleasure!"

Peace, thus repulsed, turned sadly away; and Self-Denial, wounded by Shalmanezer's rude rejection, bowed his head in silent sorrow and disappeared from the scene.

As Peace departed, Shalmanezer eagerly grasped the cup of Pleasure and pressed it to his lips, while she clasped her hand in his and said in a most charming manner, "Follow me;" and then he went willingly to the place where she dwelt.

As Shalmanezer approached the palace of Pleasure he heard the sweetest music rising on the air in magnificent swells or sinking in ravishing cadences; at his feet were springing the brightest and fairest flowers; the sweetest perfumes were bathing the air with the most exquisite fragrance; beautiful girls moved like visions of loveliness through the mazy dance; rare old wines sparkled on the festal board; the richest viands and most luscious fruits tempted the taste; and laughter, dance and song filled the air with varied delights. For a while Shalmanezer was enraptured with the palace of Pleasure. But soon he became weary of its gay confusion. The merry ripples of laughter lost their glad freshness; the once delightful music seemed to faint into strange monotones—whether the defect was in his ear or in the music he could not tell, but somehow it had ceased to gratify him; the constant flow of merry talk grew strangely distasteful to him; the pleasant viands began to pall upon his taste; at times he thought he detected a bitterness in the rare old wines which Pleasure ever and anon presented to his lips, and he turned wearily away from everything that had pleased his taste or had charmed and entranced his senses.

Shalmanezer sat moodily wishing that Desire would return and bring with him another attendant to whom he had been introduced when he had first clasped hands with Pleasure, and whose name was Wealth. While he was musing, he lifted up his eyes and saw Wealth and Desire standing at the door of his Boudoir, and near them he saw the sweet loving face of Peace, who was attended by Self-Denial. Peace was about to approach him, but he repulsed her with an impatient frown, and turning to Desire he said:

"I have grown weary of Pleasure, and I wish to be introduced to the halls of Wealth."

Taller, graver and less fair was Wealth, than her younger sister, Pleasure. If the beauty of Pleasure could be compared to the vernal freshness of Spring—that of Wealth suggested the maturity of golden harvests, and ripe autumnal fruits. Like Pleasure, she was very richly attired; a magnificent velvet robe fell in graceful folds around her well-proportioned form; like prisms of captured light, the most beautiful jewels gleamed and flashed in her hair; a girdle of the finest and most exquisitely wrought gold was clasped around her waist; her necklace and bracelets were formed of the purest jewels and finest diamonds.—But there was something in her face which betokened a want which all her wealth could not supply. There was a mournful restlessness in her eye that at times seemed to border on the deepest sadness; and yet, there was something so alluring in her manner, so dazzling in her attire, and fascinating in her surroundings, that men would often sacrifice time, talent, energy, and even conscience and manhood, to secure her smiles and bask in her favor.

"Shalmanezer," said Desire to Wealth, "has grown weary of thy sister, Pleasure, and would fain dwell in thy stately halls. Is there aught to hinder him from being one of thy favored guests?"

"Nothing at all," said Wealth, smiling. "The rich inheritance left him by his father has been increasing in value, and I am glad that he was too wise to throw in Pleasure's cup life's richest gifts away."

With these words she reached out her jewelled hand to Shalmanezer and said, "Follow me!"

Weary of the halls of Pleasure, Shalmanezer gladly rose to follow Wealth. As he was leaving, he paused a moment to bid adieu to Pleasure. But she was so changed, that he did not recognize in the faded woman with the weary, listless manner, dull eyes and hollow cheeks, the enchanting girl, who, a few years before, had led him to her halls a welcome and delighted guest. All was so changed. It seemed more like a dream than a reality, that he had dwelt for years in what now seemed like a disenchanted palace. The banquet table was strewn with broken and tasteless fragments; the flowers had lost their fragrance and beauty, and lay in piles of scentless leaves; the soft sweet music had fainted into low breathed sighs, and silence reigned in the deserted halls where dance and revelry and song had wreathed with careless mirth the bright and fleeting hours.

"Come," said Wealth, "my Chariot waits thee at the door."

Without one pang of regret, Shalmanezer turned from the halls of Pleasure, to ride with Wealth in her magnificent chariot.

As they drove along, Wealth showed Shalmanezer the smoke rising from a thousand factories. Pausing a moment, she said:—"I superintend these works and here are my subjects."

Shalmanezer gazed on the colossal piles of brick and mortar, as those castles of industry met his eye. Just then the bell rang, and he saw issuing from amid the smoke and whir of machinery a sight that filled his soul with deep compassion.

There were pale, sad-looking women wending their way home to snatch some moment's rest, and an humble meal before returning to their tasks. There were weary-looking men, who seemed to be degenerating in mental strength and physical vigor. There were young children who looked as if the warm fresh currents of life in their veins had been touched with premature decay. And saddest of all—he saw young girls who looked as if they were rapidly changing from unsophisticated girlhood into over-ripe womanhood.

"Are these thy servants?" said Shalmanezer, sadly.

"These," said Wealth, "are my servants, but not my favorites. In dark mines—close factories—beneath low roofed huts—they dig the glittering jewels, and weave the webs of splendor and beauty with which I adorn my favorites. But I see that the sight pains thee. Let us pass on to fairer scenes."

Bending down to her finely-liveried coachman, she whispered in his ear, and in a few minutes the factories, with their smoke and din, were left behind. Beautiful lawns, lovely parks, and elegant residences rose before the pleased eyes of Shalmanezer; beautiful children sported on the lawns; lovely girls roamed in the parks; and the whole scene was a bright contrast to those he had left behind.

At length they rode up an avenue of stately trees, and stopped at the home of Wealth. "Here is my dwelling," she said, "enter and be my welcome guest."

Shalmanezer accepted the invitation, and entering, gazed with delighted wonder on the splendor and beauty of the place. On the walls hung most beautiful pictures surrounded by the richest frames—rare creations of the grand old masters; lovely statues suggested the idea of life strangely imprisoned in marble; velvet carpets sank pleasantly beneath his tread; elegant book cases, inlaid with ivory and pearl, held on the shelves the grand and noble productions of the monarchs of mind who still rule from their graves in the wide realms of thought and imagination. In her halls were sumptuous halls for feasting; delightful alcoves for thought and meditation; lovely little boudoirs for cozy chats with cherished friends. Even religion found costly bibles and splendidly embossed prayer books in the chambers of repose, where beneath the softened light of golden lamps, the children of Wealth sank to rest on beds of down.

"Surely," said Shalmanezer, "he must be a strangely restless creature, who cannot be satisfied in this home of beauty, grace and affluence." And yet, while he spake, he was conscious of a sense of unrest. He tried to shake it off, but still it would return. He would find himself sighing amid the fairest scenes—oppressed with a sense of longing for something he could not define. His eye was not satisfied with seeing, nor his ear with hearing. It seemed as if life had been presented to him as a luscious fruit, and he had eagerly extracted its richest juices, and was ready to throw away the bitter rind in hopeless disgust.

While he sat gloomily surveying the past, and feeling within his soul a hunger which neither Wealth nor Pleasure could appease, he lifted his eyes towards a distant mountain whose summit was crowned with perpetual snows, although a thousand sunbeams warmed and cheered the vale below. As he gazed, he saw a youth with a proud gait, buoyant step and flashing eye, climbing the mount. In his hand he held a beautifully embossed card, on which was written an invitation from Fame to climb her almost inaccessible heights and hear the sweetest music that ever ravished mortal ear. As the youth ascended the mount, Shalmanezer heard the shouts of applause which were wafted to the ears of the young man, who continued to climb with unabated ardor.

"Here," said Shalmanezer, "is a task worthy of my powers. I have wasted much of my time in the halls of Pleasure; I have grown weary of the stately palaces of Wealth; I will go forth and climb the heights of Fame, and find a welcome in the sun-crowned palaces of Renown. O, the sight of that young man inspires my soul, and gives new tone and vigor to my life. I will not pause another moment to listen to the blandishments of Wealth. Instead of treading on these soft carpets, I will brace my soul to climb the rugged heights to gaze upon the fair face of Fame."

Just as he was making this resolve, he saw Peace and her attendant gazing anxiously and silently upon him. His face flushed with sudden anger; a wrathful light flashed from his eyes; and turning his face coldly from Peace, he said: "I do wish Peace would come without her unwelcome companion—Self-Denial I do utterly and bitterly hate." Peace again repulsed, turned sadly away, followed by Self-Denial. With eager haste Shalmanezer rose up and left the bowers of Ease and halls of Pride, to tread the rugged heights of Fame, with patient, ready feet. As he passed upward, new vigor braced his nerves. He felt an exhilaration of spirits he had never enjoyed in the halls of Wealth or bowers of Pleasure. Onward and upward he proudly moved, as the multitude, who stood at the base, cheered him with rapturous applause, and no music was ever so sweet to his ear as the plaudits of the crowd; but, as he ascended higher and higher, the voices of the multitude grew fainter and fainter; some voices that cheered him at the beginning of his journey had melted into the stillness of death; others had harshened into the rough tones of disapprobation; others were vociferously applauding a new aspirant who had since started to climb the summit of Renown; but, with his eye upon the palace of Fame, he still climbed on, while the air grew rarer, and the atmosphere colder. The old elasticity departed from his limbs, and the buoyancy from his spirits, and it seemed as if the chills of death were slowly creeping around his heart. But still, with fainter step he kept climbing upward, until almost exhausted, he sank down at the palace-gate of Fame, exclaiming, "Is this all?"

Very stately and grand was the cloud-capped palace of Fame. The pillars of her lofty abode were engraven with the names of successful generals, mighty conquerors, great leaders, grand poets, illustrious men and celebrated women. There were statues on which the tooth of Time was slowly gnawing; the statues of men whose brows had once been surrounded by a halo of glory, but were now darkened by the shadow of their crimes. Those heights which had seemed so enchanting at a distance, now seemed more like barren mounds, around which the chills of Death were ever sweeping.

Fame heard the voice of her votary, and came out to place upon his brow her greenest bays and brightest laurels, and bid him welcome to her palace; but when she saw the deathly whiteness of his face, she shrank back in pity and fear. The light was fading from his eye; his limbs had lost their manly strength; and Fame feared that the torpor of Death would overtake him before she could crown him as her honored guest. She bent down her ear to the sufferer, and heard him whisper slowly, "Peace! Peace!"

Then said Fame to her servants, "Descend to the vale, bring the best medical skill ye can find, and search for Peace, and entreat her to come; tell her that one of my votaries lies near to death, and longs for her presence." The servants descended to the vale, and soon returned, bringing with them a celebrated physician.—Peace had heard the cry of Shalmanezer, and had entered the room with her companion before the doctor had come. When the physician saw Shalmanezer, he gazed anxiously upon him, felt the fluttering pulse, and chafed the pale cold hands to restore the warmth and circulation.

In the meantime, Pleasure and Wealth having heard the story of Shalmanezer's illness, entered the room. "There is but one thing," said the physician, "can save Shalmanezer's life: some one must take the warm healthy blood from his veins and inject it into Shalmanezer's veins before he can be restored to health."

Pleasure and Wealth looked aghast when they heard the doctor's prescription. Pleasure suddenly remembered that she had a pressing engagement; Wealth said "I am no longer young, nor even well, and am sure I have not one drop of blood to spare;" Fame pitied her faithful votary, but amid the cold blasts that swept around her home, was sure it would be very imprudent for her to attempt to part with so much blood. Just as Pleasure, Wealth and Fame had refused to give the needed aid, Desire entered the room, but when he heard the conditions for the restoration of Shalmanezer, shrank back in selfish dismay, and refused also.

As Shalmanezer lay gasping for breath, and looking wistfully at his old companions, Peace, attended by Self-Denial, drew near the sick man's couch. Shalmanezer opened his eyes languidly, and closed them wearily; when life was like a joyous dream, he had repulsed Peace and utterly hated Self-Denial, and what could he dare hope from either in his hour of dire extremity. While he lay with his eyes half-closed, Self-Denial approached the bedside, and baring his arm, said to the doctor:

"Here is thy needed remedy. Take the blood from these veins, and with it restore Shalmanezer to health and strength."

The doctor struck his lancet into Self-Denial's arm, and drawing from it the needed quantity of blood, injected it into Shalmanezer's veins. The remedy was effectual. Health flushed the cheeks of Shalmanezer, and braced each nerve with new vigor, and he soon recovered from his fearful exhaustion. Then his heart did cleave unto Self-Denial. He had won his heart by his lofty sacrifice. He had bought his love by the blood from his own veins. Clasping hands with Self-Denial, he trod with him the paths of Peace, and in so doing, received an amount of true happiness which neither Pleasure, Wealth nor Fame could give.

OUT IN THE COLD.

Out in the cold mid the dreary night, Under the eaves of homes so bright; Snowflakes falling o'er mother's grave Will no one rescue, no one save?

A child left out in the dark and cold, A lamb not sheltered in any fold, Hearing the wolves of hunger bark, Out in the cold! and out in the dark.

Missing to-night the charming bliss, That lies in the mother's good-night kiss; And hearing no loving father's prayer, For blessings his children all may share.

Creeping away to some wretched den, To sleep mid the curses of drunken men And women, not as God has made, Wrecked and ruined, wronged and betrayed.

Church of the Lord reach out thy arm, And shield the hapless one from harm; Where the waves of sin are dashing wild Rescue and save the drifting child.

Wash from her life guilt's turbid foam, In the fair haven of a home; Tenderly lead the motherless girl Up to the gates of purest pearl.

The wandering feet which else had strayed, From thorny paths may yet be stayed; And a crimson track through the cold dark night May exchange to a line of loving light.

SAVE THE BOYS.

Like Dives in the deeps of Hell I cannot break this fearful spell, Nor quench the fires I've madly nursed, Nor cool this dreadful raging thirst. Take back your pledge—ye come too late! Ye cannot save me from my fate, Nor bring me back departed joys; But ye can try to save the boys.

Ye bid me break my fiery chain, Arise and be a man again, When every street with snares is spread, And nets of sin where'er I tread. No; I must reap as I did sow. The seeds of sin bring crops of woe; But with my latest breath I'll crave That ye will try the boys to save.

These bloodshot eyes were once so bright; This sin-crushed heart was glad and light; But by the wine-cup's ruddy glow I traced a path to shame and woe. A captive to my galling chain, I've tried to rise, but tried in vain— The cup allures and then destroys. Oh! from its thraldom save the boys.

Take from your streets those traps of hell Into whose gilded snares I fell. Oh! freemen, from these foul decoys Arise, and vote to save the boys. Oh ye who license men to trade In draughts that charm and then degrade, Before ye hear the cry, Too late, Oh, save the boys from my sad fate.

NOTHING AND SOMETHING.

It is nothing to me, the beauty said, With a careless toss of her pretty head; The man is weak if he can't refrain From the cup you say is fraught with pain. It was something to her in after years, When her eyes were drenched with burning tears, And she watched in lonely grief and dread, And startled to hear a staggering tread.

It is nothing to me, the mother said; I have no fear that my boy will tread In the downward path of sin and shame, And crush my heart and darken his name. It was something to her when that only son From the path of right was early won, And madly cast in the flowing bowl A ruined body and sin-wrecked soul.

It is nothing to me, the young man cried: In his eye was a flash of scorn and pride; I heed not the dreadful things ye tell: I can rule myself I know full well. It was something to him when in prison he lay The victim of drink, life ebbing away; And thought of his wretched child and wife, And the mournful wreck of his wasted life.

It is nothing to me, the merchant said, As over his ledger he bent his head; I'm busy to-day with tare and tret, And I have no time to fume and fret. It was something to him when over the wire A message came from a funeral pyre— A drunken conductor had wrecked a train, And his wife and child were among the slain.

It is nothing to me, the voter said, The party's loss is my greatest dread; Then gave his vote for the liquor trade, Though hearts were crushed and drunkards made. It was something to him in after life, When his daughter became a drunkard's wife And her hungry children cried for bread, And trembled to hear their father's tread.

Is it nothing for us to idly sleep While the cohorts of death their vigils keep? To gather the young and thoughtless in And grind in our midst a grist of sin? It is something, yes, all, for us to stand Clasping by faith our Saviour's hand; To learn to labor, live and fight On the side of God and changeless light.

WANDERER'S RETURN.

My home is so glad, my heart is so light, My wandering boy has returned to-night. He is blighted and bruised, I know, by sin, But I am so glad to welcome him in.

The child of my tenderest love and care Has broken away from the tempter's snare; To-night my heart is o'erflowing with joy, I have found again my wandering boy.

My heart has been wrung with a thousand fears, Mine eyes been drenched with the bitterest tears; Like shadows that fade are my past alarms, My boy is enclasped in his mother's arms.

The streets were not safe for my darling child; Where sin with its evil attractions smiled. But his wandering feet have ceased to roam, And to-night my wayward boy is at home—

At home with the mother that loves him best, With the hearts that have ached with sad unrest, With the hearts that are thrilling with untold joy Because we have found our wandering boy.

In that wretched man so haggard and wild I only behold my returning child, And the blissful tears from my eyes that start Are the overflow of a happy heart.

I have trodden the streets in lonely grief, I have sought in prayer for my sole relief; But the depths of my heart to-night are stirred, I know that the mother's prayer has been heard.

If the mother-love be so strong and great For her child, sin-weary and desolate, Oh what must the love of the Father be For souls who have wandered like you and me!

"FISHERS OF MEN."

I had a dream, a varied dream: Before my ravished sight The city of my Lord arose, With all its love and light.

The music of a myriad harps Flowed out with sweet accord; And saints were casting down their crowns In homage to our Lord.

My heart leaped up with untold joy; Life's toil and pain were o'er; My weary feet at last had found The bright and restful shore.

Just as I reached the gates of light, Ready to enter in, From earth arose a fearful cry Of sorrow and of sin.

I turned, and saw behind me surge A wild and stormy sea; And drowning men were reaching out Imploring hands to me.

And ev'ry lip was blanched with dread And moaning for relief; The music of the golden harps Grew fainter for their grief.

Let me return, I quickly said, Close to the pearly gate; My work is with these wretched ones, So wrecked and desolate.

An angel smiled and gently said: This is the gate of life, Wilt thou return to earth's sad scenes Its weariness and strife,

To comfort hearts that sigh and break, To dry the falling tear, Wilt thou forego the music sweet Entrancing now thy ear?

I must return, I firmly said, The struggles in that sea Shall not reach out beseeching hands In vain for help to me.

I turned to go; but as I turned The gloomy sea grew bright, And from my heart there seemed to flow Ten thousand cords of light.

And sin-wrecked men, with eager hands, Did grasp each golden cord; And with my heart I drew them on To see my gracious Lord.

Again I stood beside the gate. My heart was glad and free; For with me stood a rescued throng The Lord had given me.

SIGNING THE PLEDGE.

Do you see this cup—this tempting cup— Its sparkle and its glow? I tell you this cup has brought to me A world of shame and woe.

Do you see that woman sad and wan? One day with joy and pride, With orange blossoms in her hair, I claimed her as my bride.

And vowed that I would faithful prove Till death our lives should part; I've drenched her soul with floods of grief, And almost crushed her heart.

Do you see that gray-haired mother bend Beneath her weight of years? I've filled that aged mother's eyes With many bitter tears.

Year after year for me she prays, And tries her child to save; I've almost brought her gray hairs down In sorrow to the grave.

Do you see that boy whose wistful eyes Are gazing on my face? I've overshadowed his young life With sorrow and disgrace.

He used to greet me with a smile, His heart was light and glad; I've seen him tremble at my voice, I've made that heart so sad.

Do you see this pledge I've signed to-night? My mother, wife, and boy Shall read my purpose on that pledge And smile through tears of joy.

To know this night, this very night, I cast the wine-cup down, And from the dust of a sinful life Lift up my manhood's crown.

The faded face of my young wife With roses yet shall bloom, And joy shall light my mother's eyes On the margin of the tomb.

I have vowed to-night my only boy, With brow so fair and mild, Shall not be taunted on the streets, And called a drunkard's child.

Never again shall that young face Whiten with grief and dread, Because I've madly staggered home And sold for drink his bread.

This strong right arm unnerved by rum Shall battle with my fate; And peace and comfort crown the home By drink made desolate.

Like a drowning man, tempest-tossed, Clings to a rocky ledge, With trembling hands I've learned to grasp The gospel and the pledge.

A captive bounding from my chain, I've rent each hateful band, And by the help of grace divine A victor hope to stand.